Welcome to the
Quantum Upgrade Book Series

You may have already learned a writing process in school. But most of the time what you really need is a writing *product* – an A-paper, an impressive report, a challenging essay. The word *product* is a proud way to think of your writing: Whenever you write, you produce something. That product is *you*, in writing. For most school writing you need to complete something and send it out, or turn it in. You need a finished product, and – if you're like a lot of people – you probably need it by tomorrow morning!

Capturing your best ideas in your writing is a *POWerful* experience – one that we'd all like to have more often. This book will help you create a finished writing product by putting the *POW!* into your process with a four-step system that works – Prime It, Organize It, Write It and Wow It!

In today's quantum world, you need to be ready with fast skills and vast knowledge to learn more, be more and do more. Use this writing upgrade to expand your ideas and get the results you want out of school and life.

The Quantum Upgrade Book Series:

Quantum Learner
Quantum Reader
Quantum Writer
Quantum Memorizer
Quantum Thinker
Quantum Note-Taker

D0963680

QUANTUM WRITER

Write Easily, Less Stress,
Better Results

LEARNING FORUM PUBLICATIONS

Published by Learning Forum Publications

Submit all requests for reprinting to:

Learning Forum Publications
1938 Avenida del Oro
Oceanside, CA 92056
(760) 722-0072

Cover and interior design: Stephen Schildbach
Illustrations: Jonathan Fischer
Book concept: John Pederson
Editor: Sue Baechler

Library of Congress Control Number: 2006940416

ISBN-10: 0-945525-43-5
ISBN-13: 978-0-945525-43-1

Printed in the United States of America

To the Quantum Learner who wants to learn more,
be more and do more in school and life.

Enjoy all six of our books:
Quantum Learner, Quantum Reader,
Quantum Writer, Quantum Memorizer,
Quantum Thinker and Quantum Note-Taker.

Contents

Write Easily, Less Stress, Better Results   **1**
Becoming a Quantum Writer

Chapter 1: Prime It   **7**

Chapter 2: Organize It   **19**

Chapter 3: Write It   **27**

Chapter 4: Wow It!   **47**

Congratulations!
You're a Quantum Writer   **57**

Write Easily, Less Stress, Better Results
Becoming a Quantum Writer

What do you think of when you hear the expression
"*POW!*"? For me it's an action frame from a cartoon
strip and the word *POW*er. Whatever
thoughts and ideas pop into your
mind, chances are, they feel fast,
strong and in control – *POW!*

Ease, *POW*er and
satisfaction – that's
how writing should
feel. And that's how
it will feel to you as
a quantum writer.
You'll gain confidence
knowing that you can
succeed at any writing
assignment or opportu-
nity with a system that
gets you results.

But the expression *POW!* does more than describe
how it feels to be a quantum writer; it also represents
the four-step system that you can use to become
one yourself.

POW! SYSTEM		POW! STRATEGIES	
P	Prime It	Cluster	Fastwrite
O	Organize It	Mind Map	Frame
W	Write It	Target	Draft
!	Wow It	Creative WOW	Critic WOW

P – **Prime It** – Prime your mind; cluster and fastwrite ideas and main points.

O – **Organize It** – Organize your main points into a Mind Map and a frame.

W – **Write It** – Focus on your writing target and write a draft.

! – **Wow It!** – Optimize your writing; make it stand out.

The results you'll get from using this *POWerful* system are better grades, less stress, and more control of how you choose to spend your time. But getting the results you want means getting the practice you need. Whether it's writing or running, you need to prepare and plan if you want to do your best and enjoy the experience. The more you do it, the easier it is and the faster you become. Some days you don't want to run, but you do it anyway. You train your mind to ignore the resistance with regular exercise, and eventually, you love it. That's how writing works too. Once you get moving, and put a little *POW!* into your process, you'll wonder what took you so long to get started.

The POW! system works for any writing product – a formal essay, presentation, personal reflection, report, email message, story, article, book, etc.

For many of us, getting started is the most difficult part of writing. That's because we hear two voices at the starting line of any writing opportunity or assignment. The first is our creative voice, which is supportive and imaginative, constantly encouraging us to try out new ideas. The second voice – the louder one – is the inner critic. This voice points out each structural mistake, grammatical error, and repetitive idea.

But when you're just starting to write, these two voices are sort of like having two coaches telling you what to do at the same time. One is saying "Go get 'em!" That's the creative voice. While the other – the critic – is shouting, "Whoa, slow down!" The critic can be helpful because that's also the voice that says, "Wow, you have a lot of good ideas here. Make sure you're expressing them clearly!" You'll want to listen to your critic voice whenever it's time to edit. But you'll never get out of the starting blocks if you listen to the critic at the beginning of your writing process. Maybe that's why they call it "writer's block"!

One of the greatest things about writing is that you get to wear both a creative hat and a critic hat – lifetime success skills that you'll use in the four steps of the POW! System.

Creative Hat   Critic Hat

The first step of the quantum writer *POW!* system is **Prime It** – tune into your creative voice by priming your mind and getting your ideas down on the page.

Chapter 1:

Príme It

```
┌─────────────────────────────┐
│                             │
└─────────────────────────────┘
```

Your upgrade is in progress

Have you ever found yourself staring at a computer screen or a blank piece of paper, waiting for the words to come?

When it's time to write, whether we're excited or stressed, many of us find ourselves looking at a blank page or screen, just trying to get something started. It feels sort of like staring at a fuzzy TV screen waiting for the reception to kick in. Sometimes we know exactly what we want to write, but for some reason, it doesn't make sense when we try to write it down. And sometimes, we just don't know how to organize all of our material or ideas and turn them into a written product.

We've all experienced these moments when there seems to be a gap between the ideas in our head and the ones on the page. Many of us get stuck in the gap, and we struggle to move forward. But you can avoid this stressful and time-wasting part of writing by using two *POW!* strategies to brainstorm and record your ideas right onto your paper: **Cluster** and **Fastwrite**.

Despite what it sounds like, a brainstorm is not a downpour of brain matter! It's a way to prime your mind, let loose your creative energy, and fill the page with ideas you can use right away. These two quantum writer strategies are a lot of fun, and they're critical to your success because they put an end to writer's block forever!

POW! Step 1: P=Prime It
Two strategies to brainstorm and record your ideas on paper quickly and easily:

Cluster   **Fastwrite**

Your creative hat is most useful for Step 1, but keep your critic hat handy to edit all the ideas from your cluster.

Cluster Strategy

I first learned to cluster years ago and use it just about every time I have to write anything important. The cluster strategy works really well to generate and capture your best ideas.

A cluster is a visual representation of the way your mind sorts information. Clustering is the process of generating ideas, images and feelings around a key word or central idea. You write words and ideas that come to mind. Each word you write makes more thoughts tumble out. This process expands your list of words and ideas for writing and often helps you see patterns that help you further develop your ideas.

Professional writers have been using and teaching clustering for over three decades. In fact, you might have already learned this strategy in school. This upgrade is not always about learning something new; it's about knowing how to use strategies like clustering to write more easily and get better results by getting off to a successful start!

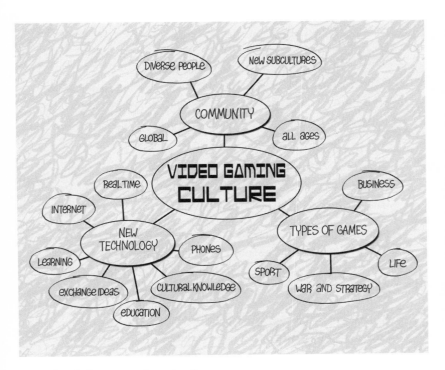

Here's how – take a look:

Notice how the subject, Video Gaming Culture, is written in the middle of the page with a circle around it. This is usually the title or main idea of what you're writing about. All the related ideas appear around the subject with circles and lines connecting them to the main idea. Secondary ideas that were sparked by these words fill the rest of the space.

Think of a writing opportunity or assignment you will need to work on soon. Get started now by making a cluster of your ideas.

Try it out:

- Take out a blank sheet of paper.

- Turn the page horizontally and write your main topic in a key word or phrase in the middle. Draw a circle around it.

- Jot down all the related ideas that you can think of, clustering them around your central thought. Draw a circle around each word or idea as you write it, and draw a line to the central thought.

- Write down any secondary ideas that were sparked by these words and again circle them, this time drawing a line to the word that sparked the idea. Repeat the first three steps until you run out of ideas.

- Allow the spokes and circles of your cluster to be free flowing. You'll organize them later.

You'll notice that the lines of the cluster loosely resemble the spokes of a bicycle wheel. This wheel may not spin in a perfect circle, but it will still help you get rolling!

See It, Say It, Draw It

Sometimes your creative mind needs some warming up to brainstorm your ideas for writing. You can prime your creative mind at any time with this See It, Say It, Draw It exercise.

See It

To accurately describe something in words, you must first observe or "see" it carefully. In other words, good writers are also good observers. Take a few seconds to study your surroundings. When you're ready, close your eyes and picture as many details as possible: the clock on your desk, your favorite poster, an empty wastebasket – whatever you can remember.
Recreate the scene in your mind.

Now pick a unique item, one you may not have noticed before, like a crack in the wall or a fortune cookie. Make up a story about that item by being curious and asking questions like: How did that item get there? Who made it? When was it made? What is it for? The more ridiculous your answers, the better! For example, maybe you imagine one big fortune cookie factory where all the world's fortune cookies are made, and the message in this particular cookie

13

was wrapped up just for you in that factory and delivered to your desk as a clue to how the rest of your life was going to turn out. *Now, take a minute to make a story for a different item in your room. It may seem silly at first, but this exercise will prime your creative mind.*

Say It

Take a closer look at the item you chose for your story. This time, describe everything you can about its actual appearance. Be as specific as possible. For example, let's say you chose a pencil on your desk. Pick it up, and talk about it. You might say: It's yellow with a few chew marks near the end. It has a tiny pinkish-tan eraser, little blue dots around the rim, weighs about two ounces, smells like dog fur, and has the word Castell on it. Hey, maybe there's a big pencil-making factory, too! *Now describe the item you selected.*

Draw it

Drawing the item from your story will further boost your observation skills by helping your mind remember more details. Like the See It and Say It parts of the exercise, drawing a picture is all about narrowing the gap between your thoughts and your writing by getting your mind ready to move, maneuver and make the jump to the page. Your picture stimulates new words and ideas you can use for your writing. *Make a drawing of the item you selected and described.*

Fastwrite Strategy

Fastwrite is exactly like it sounds. You write your ideas down very quickly just as they come out of your mind. It's the second strategy for priming your mind and turning up the volume of your creative voice, so you can cruise full speed ahead into your writing. It's easier than you think.

 First, get out your critic hat and take a few minutes to review your cluster. Cross out the ideas that you don't want to use and star your main points. Number your ideas (except those you crossed out) in the order you want them to appear in your draft. Don't worry if the order changes when you write.

15

 Now that you have prioritized your cluster of ideas, put on your creative hat again, and get ready to fastwrite. Review these tips and examples before you begin.

Fastwrite Tips:

• Consider using the starred topics of your cluster to start your sentences.

• Imagine you're surfing the Internet flowing from page to page, jotting down the information that interests you before linking to related ideas.

• Don't make changes or corrections, just go – and don't start over.

• Forget punctuation, grammar and spelling. Remember: You're not listening to the critic.

- Write whatever comes to mind as quickly as you can.

- Don't worry if your thoughts wander, just keep them flowing and don't stop until you've completely run out of ideas.

Fastwrite example:

Video gaming communities are a new subculture of diverse people. I think this is positive There's _____ and with new technology like internet and expanded boundaries and global communities and people everywhere. All ages playing and interacting. What else should I say???? What are the facts? Where do I get them?? Mention that Swedish co & that games aren't just about war or sports – solve problems. Dad would like this. Does he like to play games??? New technology and real-time play but how much exchange? Cultural knowledge shared? FIND STATISTICS! What else what else what else... Future of video game tech is so exciting. All kinds of ideas. Effect on communities of players. Need examples.

Try it out:

Pick up a pen, or open a new document on your computer and start your fastwrite. Although it's messy, a fastwrite will prime your mind and jump-start your writing process. The fastwrite strategy gives you something to work with, and the ideas came from your cluster, so you're off to a confident start.

The next step in the *POW!* System is organizing your ideas so you can see them, and turning them into paragraphs that soon become your draft.

Chapter 2:

Organize It

Your upgrade is 25% complete

Now that you have all your best ideas down on the page, you want to organize them to reach your reader with clarity and *POW*er. This is where you step back, take a look at your brainstormed ideas, and structure what you're going to write using two organizing strategies: **Mind Map**® and **Frame**.

POW! Step 2: O=Organize It
Two strategies to organize your brainstorms into what you want to write:

Mind Map

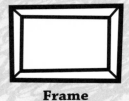

Frame

Use your creative hat in Step 2 to organize your writing.

Mind Map® Strategy

As you may already know, Tony Buzan first developed this note-taking strategy as a better way to picture, associate and expand ideas. Today, many professional writers use Mind Maps to organize and connect what they want to write. Creating a Mind Map starts with asking yourself questions about your central idea and main points.

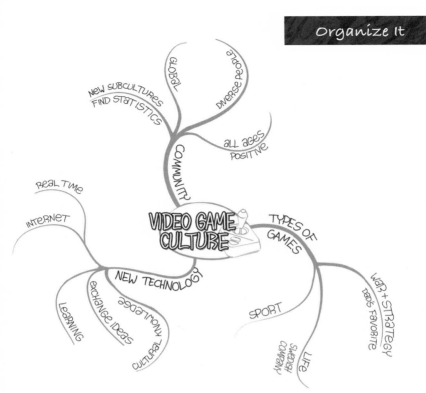

You'll find that your brain naturally wants to fill in the details and complete your map.

Take a look at the Mind Map above. Notice how it starts with a central idea and branches out to include main ideas, details and examples. You can circle the central idea, make it bold, or even create an image of it to make its meaning stand out. Draw branches from thick to thin; thicker branches for main ideas to emphasize their importance, and thinner branches for details and examples. Keep in mind that the main branches are usually different colors, although this book is printed in black and white. You can reuse colors if you need to – just not next to one another.

Try it out:

Make your own Mind Map from your cluster diagram. Your Mind Map can be a blueprint for your entire writing product. It's not a precise map, but it will help you organize your ideas and see the connections between them. It makes it easier to see your key points in chunks that support your main idea.

Frame Strategy

 Your Mind Map helped you see the big picture of how your ideas fit together. The frame strategy helps you build strong paragraphs that thoughtfully develop your ideas, and guide your reader through your writing. A strong paragraph has a main idea, detail, examples and a conclusion.

Main Idea _____
Detail _____
Example:
Detail _____
Example:
Conclusion _____

The first line is the main idea. This is the key point of the entire paragraph. Your supporting detail comes next, followed by examples, and a conclusion that sums up the point of the paragraph and a few words that transition the reader to the next paragraph.

Organize your writing by locating each of these four elements – main idea, supporting detail, examples and conclusion/transition – in each of your paragraphs. Use visual cues, like colors or font styles, to identify each of these elements in your writing, and remember to take out these cues before you turn in your draft.

Look at the sample paragraph on the next page. Notice the main idea, detail, examples and conclusion by referring to the frame above, and how the writer highlighted each of them with cues like underlining to create a strong paragraph frame.

<u>File-sharing over the Internet improves the music</u> <u>industry</u>. **It enriches the variety and choices available to consumers and helps unknown bands reach new audiences.** *For example, many bands like Justin King and Zamboni provide free downloads on sites like myspace.com to promote upcoming tours and CD releases.* <u>For these bands, and thousands like</u> <u>them, file-sharing makes their contribution to the</u> <u>music world possible. It also empowers people to</u> <u>make their own music</u>.

Main Idea: *File-sharing over the Internet improves the music industry.*

> **Detail:** *Enriches choices. Helps unknown bands reach audiences.*

>> **Example:** *Justin King, Zamboni, free downloads on myspace.com*

Conclusion: *Makes musical contributions possible.* **Transition:** *Empowers music-making*

Try it out:

Use your Mind Map to create paragraph frames for your main points.

Keeping this structure in mind as you plan your writing will help you organize and develop your ideas into a draft. For example, applying the frame strategy to a particular chunk of your Mind Map may reveal that you need another example before you're ready to write that section. Framing will help you organize your writing and develop your ideas, but you will also use this strategy in the next step in the *POW!* system – Write It.

Chapter 3:
Write It

Your upgrade is 50% complete

As I mentioned earlier, getting started is often the most difficult part of the writing process. Luckily, you're past that point! You know how to prime your creative mind and brainstorm your main points into a cluster and fastwrite. And you can organize your main ideas into a Mind Map to see how the information goes together, and structure the points into a paragraph frame.

Now you'll focus your main points with the **Target Strategy** and flow your ideas together to make meaning by creating a **Draft**.

POW! **Step 3: W=Write It**
Two strategies to focus your writing and turn your
main points into a product:

Target

Draft

You'll go back and forth from your creative hat to
your critic hat in Step 3.

Target Strategy

Like the expression *POW!*, TARGET is an acronym.
Every letter stands for an important idea that you'll
want to remember. In this case the letters stand for:

Time Audience Reason Goal Excitement Tone

These keywords will help you remember six ways to
focus your main points and connect with your readers.
When you target your writing, you're more clear and
confident as you write your draft.

- **Time:** Set a time limit. Many pros work 50 minutes
  and take 10-minute breaks.

- **Audience:** Decide who you're talking to and write
  for them.

- **Reason:** Get clear on the purpose of your writing.

- **Goal:** Define the goal you want to achieve with your writing.

- **Excitement:** Ask yourself, "What excites me about this? What's in it for me?"

- **Tone:** Clarify how you want the person to feel when they read your writing.

Let's try out the target strategy. Use your creative hat and think of an upcoming writing project for a school subject or an outside interest – maybe an essay assignment or an application for a special program.

For example, let's say you're writing a letter or personal statement for a special opportunity like a scholarship or volunteer service. With this writing opportunity in mind, walk yourself through the target strategy on the left side of the table on the next page. Notice the example responses on the right side.

Target Strategy Example	
Time: Set a time limit. Pros work for 50 minutes and take 10-minute breaks.	Ask yourself how much time you have available for this task and when it's due. Break up your time into 30-minute or 50-minute chunks to get it done.
Audience: Decide who you're talking to and write for them.	Your audience is the person(s) who will select the successful candidate. You may want to find out as much as you can about them – like title, position, correct spelling of name(s) – so you can include these details in your letter.
Reason: Get clear on the purpose of what you're writing.	You're writing the letter because you believe you have the right skills and experience.
Goal: Define the goal you want to achieve with your writing.	Your goal is to get the attention of your audience and get the position or award.
Excitement: Ask yourself, "What excites me about this? What's in it for me?"	You are excited and motivated to write the letter because the opportunity is a perfect fit for your skills, talents and dreams.
Tone: Clarify how you want the person to feel when they read your writing.	You want the reader to feel respected. You want them to know you are confident and competent, without sounding egotistical.

Consider these two Target Tips on writing with the appropriate tone and getting yourself excited about your writing.

 Target Tip on TONE: What Is the Appropriate Tone?

Two of the most *POW*erful tones in writing are sincerity and respect. Humor and sarcasm may work in person, but they can often lead to confusing and embarrassing misunderstandings in our writing.

People recognize and appreciate sincere and respectful communication (whether you're writing an essay, a letter, or an email message) and will respond by returning the same to you.

For example, if you're writing a note to someone, instead of saying: *I realize you're a very busy person with lots of important events on your schedule, but I really, really hope you'll take time from your busy schedule to join us for the kick-off yearbook meeting next Thursday.*

A more appropriate tone would be: *I know you have a busy schedule, so the kick-off meeting will be brief. I hope you'll be able to attend.*

31

**Target Tip on EXCITEMENT:
"What's In It For Me?"**

To upgrade your writing skills and become a
quantum writer, you have to ask yourself, "What's in
it for me?" (or WIIFM for short, pronounced
WHIFF-EM). WIIFM is the benefit we get from our
actions. It's the question we all ask ourselves –
either consciously or subconsciously – before setting
out to do anything. From the simplest daily tasks to
big decisions, everything has to promise some degree of personal benefit, or you have no motivation
to do it. Even helping others has a degree of WIIFM
because it gives you personal and moral satisfaction.
Sometimes the WIIFM is very clear in your mind,
other times you have to look for it – or even invent it.
Either way, you need to find it because WIIFM helps
you connect to your intrinsic motivation. Intrinsic
motivation is the most effective way to get excited
about what you're writing because it's something you
want to do for yourself, not for your teacher or your
parents (that would be extrinsic motivation).
Activities that are personally rewarding, interesting
and joyful, appeal to your intrinsic motivation. You
do it because you want to. If you love a particular
class at school or a group you meet up with, you'll
show up on time and do extra things simply because
you're excited to be there. You do it because you enjoy
it. WIIFM is a great way to get yourself excited about
any writing task!

Try it out:

Look at your paragraph frames and use the target strategy to make decisions about how you will write your draft. You can make a diagram like I did on page 30, with the letters **T A R G E T** on the left and your notes on the right, if you choose.

The target strategy is a fast, smart way to focus your writing and save yourself time and stress when you get to the next step – writing your draft.

Draft

When you have focused your writing with the target strategy, you're ready to write your draft and add some polish. You're going to be amazed at how quickly your writing comes together.

To write your draft, it's a good idea to refer to your Mind Map or paragraph frames (or both). Number the

main ideas on the map in the order you want them on your draft. Then get them down on paper. If you made paragraph frames for any of the main ideas, you can use those in your draft.

GLOBAL

DIVERSE people

NEW SUBCULTURES

FIND STATISTICS

all ages POSITIVE

COMMUNITY

VIDEO GAME CULTURE

Numbered Mind Map	Paragraph Frame
REAL TIME · INTERNET · PHONES · LEARNING · EXCHANGE IDEAS · KNOWLEDGE · CULTURAL / VIDEO GAME CULTURE / NEW TECHNOLOGY	**Main Idea 1:** *New technology expands cultural boundaries* **Detail:** *Global interaction, no single demographic, collaborative problem solving* **Example:** *World of Warcraft® and Lineage® – more than 4 million real-time online players* **Conclusion:** *Easy online access, new global communities*
VIDEO GAME CULTURE / TYPES OF GAMES · SPORT · COMMON SHARED · LIFE · BUSINESS · WAR + STRATEGY DAD'S FAVORITE	**Main Idea 2** _____ **Detail** _____ **Example:** **Detail** _____ **Example:** **Conclusion** _____

Draft

Main Idea 1: New technology like the Internet is expanding cultural boundaries of video game playing.
Detail: Video games are no longer just for youth. People of all ages around the globe are playing, exploring, communicating, and solving problems together.
Example: As of June 2006, more than 4 million people worldwide, including my dad and me, play World of Warcraft® and Lineage® video games online.
Conclusion/Transition: The Internet makes it easy for people who enjoy video gaming to create new global communities.

Main Idea 2: _____

Detail: _____

Example: _____

Conclusion: _____

Once you put together your draft from your Mind Map and paragraph frames, you have a written product that's getting close to completion. Before you get to the final WOW! step you'll polish your draft using five techniques. These techniques help you further develop your ideas and enhance both voice and meaning in your final writing product. Use both your creative and critic hats as you polish your draft.

Draft-polishing Techniques

1. **Natural-sounding Language** – write the way people think and speak.

2. **Active Voice** – make characters in your writing "act", or make something happen.

3. **Action Verbs** – use strong verbs to bring your writing to life.

4. **Specific Language** – add a personal touch with details like names and numbers.

5. **Clear, Concise, Simple** – make every word and sentence count.

1. Natural-sounding Language

 Did you ever hear anyone say, "I can easily tell you what I want to say; I just can't write it down." This is actually a common misconception, because writing and speaking are closely linked. So why can it be so difficult to transfer our verbal communication skills to our writing? One explanation is that we are used to reading formal language in textbooks. Many of the textbooks we read in school were copied from earlier textbooks that were copied from even earlier ones. The common language when these books were printed is not the same language we use today. To our ears, it sounds formal and stilted. Since that's what we read at school, we assume that's how we're supposed to write. This expectation blocks our writing process because we're

afraid to write the way we actually think and communicate. To polish your drafts, you want to get rid of this barrier by becoming comfortable using natural-sounding writing. You can apply this technique to your writing assignments by talking your way through your Mind Map and recording what comes out. Or, pretend that you're having a conversation on the topic. How would you tell someone about it in a way they would understand? What would you say to get their attention? How would you move through the discussion to cover all your main points? Call a friend and try it out. Record the conversation or take notes by writing down key words, phrases and ideas. Notice how much clearer your thoughts flow together with words that fit your manner of speaking.

Example:

The result of the study indicates that a large number of students in the U.S. struggle with academic performance because they are not proficient in basic reading skills.

Example with natural-sounding language:

The study says many U.S. students would do better in school if they had basic reading skills.

Writing how you speak will help shut out your critic voice and improve your communication. But, sometimes you need to upgrade everyday language to ensure that you get your points across.

2. Active Voice

An active voice creates momentum in your writing.

In everyday speech you'll hear people use both active voice and passive voice as they talk. The difference between active and passive voice is the same difference that exists between active and passive people. The passive people you know just let things happen to them. Active people, on the other hand, make things happen. The same is true in writing. Passive voice delays the action. Active voice, on the other hand, takes charge and creates momentum.

How to determine whether a sentence is in active or passive voice:

• Determine the actor in the sentence.

• Decide whether the actor is doing the action (active) or the action is being done (passive).

Passive Example:

The guitar was played by the lead singer.

In this sentence, the actor (the guitar player) has been pushed to the end of the sentence, separating the actor from the action. This separation creates the impression that the action "was done," which means that the sentence is in passive voice.

Change this sentence from passive to active voice by putting the action with the actor, using the sentence order subject, verb, object.

Active Example:

The lead singer played the guitar.

Switching this sentence to the active voice accomplishes three important things:

- puts the action back where it belongs – with the actor

- tightens and shortens the sentence with the sentence order subject, verb, object

- eliminates the weak "to be" verb by replacing it with the strong, active verb "played"

3. Action Verbs

 Capture your ideas with strong active verbs. The verb serves as the central word in any sentence – the action, the part of speech that creates movement. But some verbs do this job better than others. A perfect example of a weak verb that can usually be replaced by a stronger one is the verb "to be," in all its forms: is, am, are, was, were, will be, can and should be.

Example:

Compare "Sarah was the leader of the team," with "Sarah led the team." Or what about the difference between, "I am sure that you understand my decision," and, "I trust you understand my decision."

Action Verb List			
Act	Familiarize	Manage	Save
Adapt	Figure	Master	Simplify
Address	Find	Mediate	Solve
Analyze	Focus	Mitigate	Specify
Apply	Formulate	Motivate	Stimulate
Assist			Strategize
	Gather	Navigate	Strengthen
Begin	Generate	Negotiate	Study
Brainstorm	Govern		Systematize
Budget	Guide	Observe	
Build		Obtain	Talk
	Handle	Open	Think
Calculate	Harness	Orchestrate	Transfer
Communicate	Help	Organize	Translate
Compile	Hire		Treat
Compute	Hold	Participate	Tutor
Consult		Persuade	
Coordinate	Identify	Predict	Understand
	Instruct	Promote	Unify
Define	Intend	Pronounce	Update
Describe	Invent		Upgrade
Determine		Quote	
Devise	Judge		Visualize
Distribute	Justify	Reason	Vitalize
		Recommend	
Edit	Know	Research	Warrant
Electrify		Resolve	Work
Eliminate	Lead	Retrieve	Wrangle
Enlarge	Lecture	Review	Write

You can't totally avoid weak verbs, but using more descriptive verbs, such as those on the next page, will bring your writing to life.

How do you use the action verb list? When you're reading your draft, look for weaknesses like this one: "The two inventors came up with a plan to get their new product on a popular television show." Instead of "came up with" you might substitute the word "devised". Now it's stronger and reads like this: "The two inventors devised a plan to get their new product on a popular television show."

4. Specific Language

Have you ever been standing in line for a movie or walking in the mall when someone tries to get your attention by saying, "Hey, do you know what time it is?" They're probably not trying to sound rude. They just want to know what time it is, and they don't know your name. There's no harm in that. But chances are it still strikes you in a negative way. That's because people usually react better to personalized information.

This is especially important to remember in your
writing. If you know someone's name, use it. Don't
say "they" if you mean Rachel, Daresh and Phoebe.
Instead of writing "I sent your poem to the editor of
that writing magazine," write "I sent your poem to
Judy Cassidy, the editor of Young Writers Magazine."
Whether it's names or numbers, be as specific as
possible with your descriptions. For example, instead
of writing "small fortune", use the actual amount, like
$10,000. It also helps to get rid of other vague
qualities like: *generally*, *to some degree*, and *a number of*.
Instead of saying "several people" will be at the book
club meeting, find out how many will be there and
include the exact number in your announcement.

Using specific language also means that the objective
of your writing should be clearly stated, not left for the
readers to figure out for themselves.

Remember, you can get what you want out of your
writing – but you have to be specific.

5. Keep It Clear, Concise and Simple

This final draft-polishing technique helps
you make every word and sentence count.
It's best to use sentences that contain
twenty words or less. Vary the actual
number to keep your writing interesting and fresh.
Choose small words over big ones, and keep your
paragraphs short and to the point – four to eight
sentences is a good range. You can also tighten up

your writing by looking for "wind-up" phrases at the beginning of your sentences and paragraphs. Examples of wind-up phrases are: *In the future, for the record, of the opinion.* Consider how much clearer the sentence below is without extra wind-up wording.

Example:

Contrary to what the article we read for class states, file sharing over the Internet improves the music industry.

Example without wind-up wording:

File sharing over the Internet improves the music industry.

These five techniques can be used to polish any writing, any time. Your final step in the *POW!* system gets you a finished writing product.

Chapter 4:

Wow It!

███████████████████░░░░░░

Your upgrade is 75% complete

Get ready to WOW! your writing and finish your product! You have already used the first three steps of the quantum writer system – Prime It, Organize It and Write It – to communicate your best ideas in skillful ways. At this point, you might be tempted to send in or turn in your writing. But the final step requires your creative hat to make your writing really stand out and your critic hat to check for accuracy. This step gives you two WOW! strategies – the **Creative WOW** and the **Critic WOW** – to optimize your writing and get the results you want.

POW! Step 4: !=Wow It!

Two strategies to add the spark and check your writing for accuracy.

Creative WOW

Critic WOW

Use your creative hat and critic hat to optimize your writing. And remember, you are the only one who can decide when your writing product is finished.

Creative WOW

The creative WOW! makes your writing stand out. Here are four creative WOW! techniques that add spark to your writing:

- **Show Not Tell:** create a picture in your reader's mind

- **Slo Mo:** imagine things in slow motion, then describe them in your writing

- **SPAM:** Simile, Personification, Alliteration, Metaphor

- **Crack the Clichés:** write your own words – clichés are often overused

WOW! Show Not Tell

The most effective way to communicate meaning is to create a picture in your reader's mind. Remember how you warmed up your observation skills using the See It, Say It, Draw It exercise? Apply your upgraded observation skills to your writing by showing your reader what you want them to see with descriptive language.

Example of Tell: You stand on a stage and tell a large audience what you value in your life.

Example of Show: Imagine yourself on a stage, alone in front of 100 excited kids. You're a little nervous, but determined. Then – full of confidence – you look straight ahead at the crowd and share a deep personal value.

WOW! Slow Mo

Observe and include more details by imagining things in slow motion, and then describing them in your writing. Imagine you're describing a piece of pizza. Think about the last time you ate a delicious piece of cheesy pizza. Now, imagine the experience in slow motion to recall the details that bring the experience alive in your memory.

Example: I could smell each individual ingredient as I raised the slice to my lips. My fingers and the corners of my mouth felt covered with a layer of wet grease. The hot cheese stuck to the roof of my mouth. A few pepperoni pieces slid off the top, connected by strings of cheese that I caught on their way down and put in my mouth.

WOW! SPAM

Artists use paint to show their ideas. Writers use SPAM! SPAM stands for Simile, Personification, Alliteration and Metaphor. These four ingredients will turn any so-so draft into a work of WOW!

SIMILE	Simile is a figure of speech comparing one thing to another using the words "like" or "as."
	Examples: *I powered through the assignment like a sports car with a full tank of gas. The evening was as cool as the other side of the pillow. The music shook the walls like an earthquake.*
PERSONIFICATION	Use the power of personification by giving human characteristics to things, qualities or ideas.
	Examples: *The wind ran across the sand. The blank page stared back at Ellen with an empty gaze.* The page didn't actually look at Ellen, but describing the scenario with personification will help the reader create a picture in their mind and understand your meaning.
ALLITERATION	Alliteration is the repetition of the same sound at the beginning of a series of words.
	Examples: *Four fresh footsteps in a field of flowers. A steaming Starbucks single-shot latte.* Don't force alliteration, but sprinkling it in where it works will improve the natural flow of your writing and impress your readers.
METAPHOR	Like simile, metaphor is a figure of speech that compares two things or ideas that are not usually associated to one another. However, metaphors do not use the words "like" or "as."
	Examples: *The world is a stage. Her legs were coiled springs lifting her for the rebound.*

WOW! Crack the Clichés

Clichés are common phrases used over and over again because they are familiar. Sometimes they are useful, but when you use clichés in writing, it often tells the reader that you don't care enough about the product to use your own words.

It's usually true that *lightning doesn't strike twice*. It is also true that it would be *easy as pie* to express this idea another way. But it's easy to fall back on common phrases, or clichés, in our writing. It's better to take credit for your thoughts and efforts by putting your ideas into you own words.

Instead of writing: *Many hands make for quick work* –
try: *We can get this done quickly, if we get everyone involved.*
Instead of writing: *I felt as light as a feather after the race* –
try: *I was not sore or winded after the race.*

Notice how much more descriptive and specific the writing becomes without the clichés. You don't have to take the time to say everything in an entirely new way. Sometimes it's OK to use familiar expressions because they have distinct meaning to your readers. You must tread the fine line that separates the familiar from the banal. Avoiding clichés might seem like a small detail; but remember, *a chain is only as strong as its weakest link!*

And now it's time to change hats!

Critic WOW

Put on your critic hat and tune into your critic voice. Check your draft for *accuracy,* then for *detail and examples* you may want to add or change, and then for *polishing opportunities* you might have missed or want to strengthen. Finally, *goof-proof* details like spelling, punctuation and grammar.

Accuracy

First, try three critic WOW! techniques to check your entire draft for accuracy:

1. **Read It Out Loud:** How does it sound? Is it you? You'll be surprised by how easy it is to catch mistakes, spelling errors, and optimize your wording by simply hearing your writing.

2. **Sit On It:** If you have time, walk away from your writing for a short period. This allows time for your ego to take a hike, making more room for your critic voice. If you can take a short break, you'll be more likely to read what you actually wrote, rather than what you believe you wrote.

3. **Exchange It With a Friend:**
Sometimes your creative voice is so powerful and connected to the words on the page that it refuses to let the critic take over. Exchanging your paper with a friend you trust and respect is one way to get around this problem. Use the feedback to see your draft with new eyes and discover areas for improvement.

Detail and Examples

Next, check your paragraph frames. Read each paragraph and ask yourself: *Do I have the detail and examples I need to communicate my points?* You may want to use your Mind Map or paragraph frames for reference.

Polishing Opportunities

Now recheck your draft for polishing opportunities. Ask yourself: *Did I use the five draft-polishing techniques?*

1. **Natural-sounding Language:** Did I write the way people think and speak?

2. **Active Voice:** Did I make characters "act", or make something happen?

3. **Action Verbs:** Did I use strong verbs to bring my writing to life?

4. **Specific Language:** Did I add a personal touch with details like names and numbers?

5. **Clear, Concise, Simple:** Did I make every word and sentence count?

Finally, go back and **goof-proof** your writing to be sure that spelling and punctuation mistakes don't wipe out the WOW!

WOW! Goof-Proof the Details

For the details of your writing – like spelling, punctuation and grammar – try the goof-proof techniques seen below for a final review.

Read It Backwards
This works great for short assignments, letters or emails. The mistakes jump out at you because you're reading word by word without stringing complete thoughts together.

Use Reference Material
Use dictionaries, usage handbooks, and style guides. Even the most competent writers rely on outside sources to check spelling and punctuation rules. Remember to keep your references up to date as styles and usage change.

Take Advantage of Modern Technology
Remember not to worry about the grammar, spelling and punctuation until after you've finished writing. When you are ready to check it, use the spelling and grammar programs on your computer. However, remember not to rely totally on these programs. Most spell checkers don't tell you *weather* or not you've used a homonym, a word that sounds the same but has a different meaning.

Conclusion
Now You Can Turn In That Writing Product!

I bet you're feeling pretty good about writing right now. You feel confident knowing you can *POW*er through any writing opportunity or assignment – *POW!* – with a system for ease and satisfaction. You're getting excited about the results – like clearer communication, less stress, and better grades – because you took the time to add the WOW! Now you can press the print or send button and turn in that writing product, knowing that the quantum writer in you came through again.

Your upgrade is 100% complete

Congratulations!
You're a Quantum Writer

You have just learned a *POW*erful four-step system to put the *POW!* into your writing process. A great way to practice the *POW!* system is when you have to summarize or take notes. You might even want to keep a portfolio of your writing to compare and improve.

Now every time you write something, you know how to use your creative voice and critic voice, approach it more easily, with less stress, and get a better result.

P: Prime your mind with cluster and fastwrite brainstorming strategies to get your ideas on paper. And warm up your creative voice with the See It, Say It, Draw It exercise.

O: Organize your ideas using a Mind Map and paragraph frame to add detail and examples that thoughtfully develop ideas and guide the reader through your writing.

W: Write. Use the target strategy to focus your writing, and the draft strategy to flow your Mind Map and frames into a written draft in skillful ways. The five draft-polishing techniques further enhance your voice and meaning, and get you close to a finished product: natural-sounding language, active voice, action verbs, specific language, and concise, simple and clear.

!: Wow It! Improve your ideas by putting the WOW! in your process with techniques to optimize your writing and add the spark with Show Not Tell, Slow-Mo, SPAM, Crack the Clichés, and a final Goof-Proof review.

Practice this *POW!* system to create excellent writing products without breaking a sweat. As a quantum writer, you'll get to the finish line with ease and win every time!

About the Author

Bobbi DePorter
Bobbi DePorter is the cofounder of SuperCamp and
president of Quantum Learning Network (QLN).
Based in Oceanside, California, QLN is a global
education leader impacting more than 2 million youth
and adults from 50 states and 80 countries with
programs for personal and academic excellence. Her
previous books include *Quantum Success*, *Quantum
Teaching*, *Quantum Learning* and *The Seven Biggest Teen
Problems And How To Turn Them Into Strengths*, and
have been printed in seven languages with worldwide
distribution.

Books by Bobbi DePorter

The Quantum Upgrade Series
Quantum Learner
Quantum Reader
Quantum Writer
Quantum Memorizer
Quantum Thinker
Quantum Note-Taker

Quantum Success: 8 Key Catalysts to Shift Your Energy into Dynamic Focus
Quantum Business: Achieving Success through Quantum Learning
Quantum Teaching: Orchestrating Student Success
Quantum Learning: Unleashing the Genius in You
The 8 Keys of Excellence: Principles to Live By
The Seven Biggest Teen Problems And How To Turn Them Into Strengths

How to Contact the Quantum Learning Network

By Phone: (760) 722-0072
By Mail: Quantum Learning Network
        1938 Avenida del Oro
        Oceanside, CA 92056

Online: www.QLN.com

Receive your complimentary *"I am a Quantum Learner"* poster at www.QuantumLearner.com.

International associate offices in Taiwan, China, Hong Kong, South Korea, Malaysia, Singapore, Indonesia, Mexico, Dominican Republic and Switzerland